Unstill Mosaics

The Book of Love, Loss, and Longing

James Walton

This book may get you any, or all, of those three things within the constraints of how we get there.

ISBN: 978-1-925949-10-0

Copyright © James Walton 2019

All rights reserved

No part of this publication may be reproduced, stored in a retrieval system, or transmitted in any form by any means electronic, mechanical, photocopying, recording, or otherwise, without the prior consent of the author.

Cover: Cat and Daughter
by Toshiko Mitani
with the kind permission of the owner:

and the Museum of Kyoto, Kyoto Prefecture Japan. With special thanks for the assistance of Sayoko Ueda, curator, Paintings.

For Y, whose front porch I still loiter about, waiting for flight.

My best of friends, Eileen and Peter who said I could stay for one night and let me stay forever.

Contents

sorry (i forgot your Unbirthday) e e	1
16 or 75, 46xY	2
A study of lovers and not	3
Old Falls Road	4
A Wonthaggi Coal Miner's Daughter Says	5
A Dairy Hand on a Hill	6
Wiser Men than Me	8
Whisper	9
On the Dial	10
Armada Psalm to the Spanish Main	12
Boomerang	14
Too sleepy for work in the herringbone	15
Skinning words, two-part arrivals	16
Art of Cartography	17
Under the Flinders Street Clocks	18
Crazy, Crazy Love on the Seniors Card/	19
Sideways Steam Train	19
At Cumberland River	20
Venus Bay, New Year's Day	21
Map Maker of (Number Five)	22
Tithonus and Dawn	24
Delphi Descent	26
Avignon	27
Unrequited forester contrite with sunrise	28
Birthday Stereophonics of the Elder Kind	30

Two handed draw	32
A Bandelier of Xcruciating Lovingkindness	33
Blackberry Sonnet/ The hay cutter speaks of his love	34
Thunderstorm	35
Pablo	36
Don't ask me	37
Ballooning, Yarra Valley	38
Three quarters of a time,	39
coming home with the wind	39
Sunsetted Clauses	40
DNA	41
This is a half-done fjord/wood splitting accident blues	42
Fado	43
The Full Moon	44
First, 1975	45
Abandoned soliloquy	46
Sorting the Morning	48
Free Fall	49
Roman Baths	50
Frog Love	51
quietly the light is listening	52
Graffiti, Fitzroy North, 1980	53
Potter's Wheel	54
Happy Birthday Gutsache	55
Phone Call to Sari	56
Hellespont Queens Parade Clifton Hill	57

Palliative Care	58
Here and Now/Then and There	59
Out of the Bend	60
Husk	61
Last Days of Watsonia High	62
One year I grew Navajo maize	63
Diary of Anne Boleyn	64
On the Death of a Past Love	66
I don't know what to say	67
not Another small Fucking love Poem	68
I Have Your Back	69
My Stammer Art	70
I span in a hammock	71
Bequeathable Sanitoria	72
Made in Milk	73
I wore a day as showy as	74
Love breaks	75
I'll lay down with dictionaries	76
(and you)	76
Letter to Lois	78
In Charles Street Greensborough	80
age of the Sargasso tiger	81
Near Death (Experienced Applicants Only)	82
Please Address the Selection Criteria	82
Leary Presents at the Writers Festival	84
Into the Wilderness	87

Leonard Cohen and Me, Not by the Levee	88
Now I'm Sixty-Four	90
Kissing Helen Mirren	91
Rap, rap, rap, rap, ill tidings call	92
But my lips digress	93
Wuthering	94
Truman Capote's brownstone	96
That's all, folks	97
Acknowledgements	99
About the author	101

My father Archie lived to be nearly 100. He had an older brother Bert he only saw a couple of times. Bert was politicised by his experience of World War 1, came home and became a red-hot trade unionist. Bert is James Walton's grandfather. I get my writing from Dad. So here we are, James and I, two old word-rivers with a related source sidling to the sea…....

Martin Flanagan, writer, poet, essayist, journalist, relative, waving to our shore.

sorry (i forgot your Unbirthday) e e

I like the way our bodies go
together as gelato. How my dark arm
is against your tummy, a swirl in dawn.
In that gentle spoon. The wonga vine
of your hair, black blossom in my face.
I could breathe all of you in. My lips
settle in places on your spine, or fall
away to find new things, although they've
been there, again and again. I like the night.
Its dreamy convalescence, your daggy
chequered pyjamas, my teeth
undoing the draw string of everything.

16 or 75, 46xY

I know you dislike statistics
but the missing variable
was only ever us

and if I could play
the perfect instrument
transcribe a rhapsody in volition

to sax or cello or flute
then I would be closer
to the reclaimed harmonics

of words to sounds
an arrangement of years
in an ascension that winds itself

says let's fall by unused notes
within the new composure
of all these discoveries

A study of lovers and not

as if

they have swallowed a rainbow
their gait a warble

the rest

move in tight bandages
wobble in strain
heads tilted

Moon River

Audrey Hepburn
looking in

Old Falls Road

Old Falls Road, the signs have been removed.
To keep the tourists confused. The secrete
Where dinosaur age mushrooms
Prevail against the odds.
My lips ease off timeless elastic lines,
Blue Danish goes soft in jazz.
Wine becomes warm, we sit afterwards,
Backs against the leaking rock face,
No ancient roar now,
Just the chirpy tinkling,
Of private reclaimed places
Where a lyrebird drinks.

A Wonthaggi Coal Miner's Daughter Says

see that's a hog deer print
pointing holding in a slight crouch
going down to the falls
in a hardwood plantation
how can I tell her
that no tracking can save us
there is this little while
of a freedom seen in nesting birds
or that cray sliding away
off a banking crest to deeper clime
standing up holstering her safety on
puts a finger to a lip then mine
hand against my mansplaining chest
says she doesn't follow to shoot
but likes to know where things are heading

A Dairy Hand on a Hill

I milked a season
in the high range near Timboon
for a Bavarian named Rudi,

who built a Black Forest house
out of place against eucalypts
like those old special effects,

a wobbly head stuck on the wrong body
land so fat the border collies
pretended to bring the cows in,

spent their time fossicking
in earth as black as truffle
then red in deep Shiraz.

His daughter would say
'Look the Sky pours into the Sea'
and that she didn't love me,

was going back to Germany
so tanned she'd vanish in a paddock
I had to look close to catch,

an auburn dancing shimmer
she drifted in light then flew by
left me a demijohn stranded,

a becalmed catamaran
but sometimes she wrapped me in Sienna
just for a while 'You're my Man'.

Wiser Men than Me

They say we're too old
seven decades in
but they don't know
how the Morocco
of your hair
turning to me
touching like gentle rain
coined in all the moments
others feel only once
lingers out of mornings
still to be tousled
and I fall again
into this velvet pocket
folded over and over
in a written keepsake
each bombe alaska
puzzled between thumb and promise
holds all our lively numbers
choose any one you like.

Whisper

Whisper 'Antarctica' in your love's ear
emphasise the 'c' so she knows you're serious,
sang- froid continent expansive enough
perhaps to carry the weight of sighs.

Settle around the voile of unbridled climate change
in a tangle of sheets from this break away berg,
evaporate together at the drip of exchange
lose the way back in there here.

Slippery aurora pillows sightless the blinds
have courage to stress the second 'c' aloud,
now a tropical breakfast of avocadoes
in the pineapple clasp of all melting barriers.

On the Dial

A February day
cracked by constant drizzle
like a thin glass in hot water
penguin piss that finally came
with the so often delayed Antarctic front

I'm making dhal
Jackson Browne is on loud
songs about the minimum wage
and small-town shows running late
crowds with thinned liquor and smokes

You're in the city
trammed back from Bennett's Lane
and espresso chocolate martini gigs
I've lost the sheets to the sudden gales
caught and dyed blackberry in the fifteen-acre gully

Walking the horses
laughing at the sling gate
how they stared trying to tell me
that a bark is different to a squawk
as the eagle's droopy nonchalance casts away

They swoon new grass
pass me in Miles Davis jamming
spurt their tails in plumes from paddocks
my jumper is sodden with details of Munich
your bed was next to the shower where the door opened

Humming to Love Somebody
the moss on the roof is years away
leaning on the Norfolk Pine watching snotty clouds
curdling native blueberry along the crusty valley road
trying to avoid something country and western escaping

Mr Tambourine Man creeps in
and I can't help it but my feet are moving
the fields are pages of ink dirt and parched white feed
tractors score lines dragging thistles out of a misty fleet
in a swarm of noise shallaying the truncated new horizon

I read it somewhere
the previous generation's music
imprints in hidden vacuity occupies secret places
washing through ethereal surrounds exposing intimacies
leaving you hanging a paper lantern at the end of a stick

Nina arrives suddenly
hitting a flat discord that doesn't matter
and I've caught on to a Maria Callas fly by
of such ascendant laddering through the maze of days
that I can remember the things I forgot to be who I am

Back in the kitchen
the only reception is Triple J or Classic FM
sometimes there's a crackle that hints another state
unearthed doing dishes whistling Beethoven's seventh
kilometres away the neighbour's kelpie stretches pawing
at the stations

Armada Psalm to the Spanish Main

You were more Romany than Dutch
in most of those inclinations gypsy
not polite unqizzical Amsterdam
a head of flumed unwilted magenta
a jack in the box of surprises
that could not be upbraided

I still cook for the both of us
although there's a chef travelling
with the circus in Spain
last I heard north of Barcelona
in the best of sumac and spice
the lead aerial and a mania on rope

Here I fly solo in practised anticipation
a spiral hovering where present recedes to past
buffeted and a little unsteady
arms out legs bent in a parachutist's pose
not sure the net is forgiving enough
to hold comfort in a wind tunnel of sprains

My Iberian blood sandwiched centuries ago
between an obsession of Princes
and the lure of aqua marine imaginings
forecastled and entwined as abandoned lovers
made threadbare and honest on the Irish coast
a siren that broke what was left of Seville

wandering is not only the recourse of nomads
and your laughter needed a place to land
but I miss its elegant solution
the way the hoops crash an argument
juggle and make inane the proposition in spheres
as my anchor drags its weary way home

Boomerang

I thought
I was starting
to forget

you asked me
were your eyes
different colours

being one eighth Chinese

the first kid's slide
hitting the ground
at the base

breathless but laughing
and your
hands on my ribs

in our own nebula

you're full of it
you said
and now I remember

everything

all of the pastel shades
on the Smarties packet
and the spill of a Galaxy

Too sleepy for work in the herringbone

the smell of hay
is seaweed and sex
rolled out like

washing basket ducks on a wall
falling spilled laundry clouds
your waist untangling preludes

the violin's turn at handle
my hands too naively cold
for this bow to play

the sunglasses of autumn
as trees resist winter
bees tango clover

drop and rise in saunter
these days make lazy milk
tasting of lips

and sautéed camembert

Skinning words, two-part arrivals

She came back, suddenly
   god eats your soul
At 3.47 this morning
   like a custard tart
I've learnt not to ask
   pushing the crumbs of boundary
Where she's been
   from the corners of mouths
I turn over, put my head
   a knave of bachelors
Between her shoulder and breast
   wayward as a slipped jib
The way I know she likes
   splitting out of the skein
Later she'll stir, put
   the incomplete scrabbling
Her head on my flokati chest
   where the marks dug through
Place her hand over mine
   searing in the tangled keen
Rise a little, gently
   I will come to a Holy City
Push her lips onto mine
   bathe in these cyan waters
And make me breathe again
   to make me breathe again

Art of Cartography

Trying to draw it from behind your ear
down the line to the point where,
I looked out on a harlequin sky
and my fingers learned to border that part:
Chagall's goats leapt through
The gossamer quilt of your tranquil breathing
to trespass on my lone way of shining dreamy need.
Entangled, not lost, my love sought refuge
from the undiscovered world of others.
The pilot along your breastplate leads
my now familiar tracing of the searching
ends of maps, tipping the world over again;
as the lapping sounds of dawn echo to
the watching of your gentle waking.
This is when the moment catches
my leaky vessel life is grounded,
between the ticking remonstrance
of bedside clocks reminding
that I journey these secret shoals so willingly,
taking the depth to try and fathom in the
ceaseless navigation of your mind,
the wondrous invitation of the art of cartography.

Under the Flinders Street Clocks

I am waiting

We were seventeen when you said
we'd meet under the clocks
at Flinders Street Station, each decade
for twenty years I waited for you.
Photographed by students, longingly harassed
by alms gatherers, still there the third time
that other guy, seen by everyone
in the woollen monk's habit morphed out of uni
hair unfledged as usual, held there by an umbrella

I am waiting

At the forty-year plimsoll line
new trains bringing new suburbs
of ancient peoples having traversed
the earth, I am waiting for Esperanto
to ask them all where you are.
I will be under the hands of half a century
as the new ticketing system fails again,
in the chimes of reasons the next time
to make sense of this liturgy of travail

I am waiting I am waiting still

Crazy, Crazy Love on the Seniors Card/ Sideways Steam Train

Delay the departing train
down at the rail head,
the heart has four chambers
but only one fully ticketed love.
Then spin the cylinder with gentleness
place the antique funnel of it with care,
you want this geyser single life to blow
a detonation and aftershock of lyrical candela.
Run run over the soaked platform
slide slip and screech to a rattling tin sky,
turn around the face at the blotting window
chant it breathe it grasp it at the handle.
Make the rusty stoker from the taste of cinnamon
get there scramble by the step up,
in you go trip over the stranger's stare
open the scrapbook at pages that should have stuck.
Tell her things falling apart are beginning again
of how quicksand is not a way to be cleansed,
the one-way fare was all the carriage ever needed
and you still feel its mad career
taking you beyond destination.

At Cumberland River

At Cumberland River
our love burnt itself out
we fucked ourselves senseless
there where the cabins hid away
between the declining sea and track

Now Otways fires
lick around those memories
receding into themselves unquiet
like pages of tumbling favourites loose
among mixed chapters in an unforgiving too hot wind

Blowing open blowing closed
scorched remnants have their say
dropping parachutes of silky words
trying to make a landing of pillowy remorse
where we laid bare the wide brim of what had been

Venus Bay, New Year's Day

we drive over to your sister's
on a day shiny and crisp
as porcelain
the tide wild
in a thousand Hokusai
the flags only metres apart
zinced oiled kids slosh around
sea line hallucinates
big frog clouds blurp horizons
my heart is awash
like our first kiss
I was too shy to give
a ring in tern
among the gulls
all one flight
when the eagle passes
surf club posters
Greek Indian Italian nights
ten dollars plus trivia
Mark bellows Hey Brother
a voice you can hear
all the way to Croatia
an elder has a stick
in case of snakes
joyful bevies of children run
skittish Christmas lights
splashing away of parents
teenagers baulk time
afternoon shakes free
the sun a gentle underline

Map Maker of (Number Five)

Simon sits in the paddock entrance
alone at his table with his drawings,
in his pocket a piece of cotton jade
(Number 29 of Work Team 3).

Although the State has copies
it promises to keep, he worries
New Europe doesn't want to remember,
how much love passed down that road
(Avenue 1 New Life Township).

The train station and the
lorry turnaround, carefully designed
facades of terminus settlement
all so efficiently removed.

Surprising then, they took the fence
down and he stood forgotten in the silver birches
until there was nothing, the homicidal
order disappearing under daisy chains.

These days they come to find where family
and whole villages were not recorded,
thank him for not forgetting by rolling
them up in his magic carpet of ink
(3 metre by 3 metre Chart).

And he can't say a thing but wonders
if they understand but still blame him somehow,
because a pretty girl in 1942 with sand
in her hair and sepia eyes wearing a
chartreuse pinafore,
(Stack 12 Dresses and Other Sundry Items) –

asked would it hurt much and
because he was only fifteen and could
only mumble "only for a little while",
he lives to know it's still going.

Tithonus and Dawn

do not fall in love with a God
when they say forever
it is the duration of vanity only

out of my breathless ossuary
these slow seconds
turn within themselves

a tapestry made of stone

Eos asked him to make me eternal
we were to be beautiful together
a hand aside the mouth of Zeus

his incremental curse of immortality
a hover in the white noise
of this bitter tea

once to kiss the feet of stars
no longer she breaks upon me
I do not live I do not die

locked in this closet
talking a babble of dispossession
my words hear themselves

the momentary visit of light after night
occasionally to shine on my withering
where I age in shadow forever waiting

without the strength to hold a stutter of lamp

Delphi Descent

The only thing that you will ever learn
is that love won't break your heart,
usually. Tear out those wrist lines
paint them in the blood of the goat,
carefully. When you hang me upside down
remember whether obedience or heavenly nearness,
summoned. Hands outstretched offered in peace
no longer warmed at the oracle brazier,
pray. Our pulse runs together finally
earth above a fatal dizziness spell,
ends. Burnt rosemary, a theocracy of wood,
the beautiful frailty of human souls make the gods.

Avignon

In a car park outside a walled city
where the desert ash tossed
and the plane trees drenched hay fever,
you told me you loved me
with an unquenched fury
all seasons ardent like hard rain on concrete,
more androgynous then
than Bob and Sara's Chelsea rooms
our album cover by Schiele.

I ate an avocado out of the small of your back
the lemon the salt the butter
those laughing meridians transparent parchment,
trace ways of seven decades
our conclusive equations marked
by these lines of trawling bell wethers,
now fold us in place nodding off together
dreaming of the Rosetta Stone
and the mystery in new hips.

Unrequited forester contrite with sunrise

still smouldering
with interred lightning
this tempered wilderness

life drawings of fire
dance in alphabet

hills make charcoal
smudge the outlines
saltpetre heathen tongues

peel back these veins
as gut for flamenco

in the valleys now
courts the dragon
eludes the celibate dawn

will your heart match
the wing flap

seek without shame
and make fertile
this ear drum's beat

cast lots along the razorback
to such unending desire

this true name
can only be spoken
by counting years aloud

into any inferno
I will call them out

wanting to hear
all you have again
in a quickened reprise

Birthday Stereophonics of the Elder Kind

At times my body heat
presages combustion,
but we're in the Eye of Us
this constant iridescence,
my VU bright lit
in the red corner.

Going off like radiation
a heart ticking boom,
an amplifier out of mode
but so mellow,
the bass specific
no matter how the EQ is justified.

A kid's month is a summer tortoise
the day a year of beach towels,
before the lift off
sheds stages of experience,
and you get to look back
at things beyond iteration.

Anniversary on a sky flipped decanted day
a virtuoso blue eclipse,
three sides of the circle
disappearing to bloom,
a lifetime production
full staves at intersect.

I know you prefer baroque over romantic
a cello in tune the piano pride of place,
the storm passing
but I couldn't help myself,
and not being Jim Croce
I couldn't say it in a song.

Two handed draw

I had thought
like a bird falling from a nest,
undressed as a heart
beating within my palm,
to have outlived usefulness

instead with both arms lifting
because I had no choice,
that frantic beak signing
in all the shredded shorthand,
ever lost to this binary world

placed the wingless thing
into the silky oak's airy cradle,
then sat cross legged and whistled
a feathery version of In My life,
waiting for new down to form

A Bandelier of Xcruciating Lovingkindness

by these crossed arms
the spoon of my not so supple being
arcs in your direction
unadjusted by daylight saving
our out of fashioned days linger
reading back lines no better than
these fourteen hours
of love and talk and warmth
the cloudless complexion of life apparent
beyond an end of Winter haze

Blackberry Sonnet/ The hay cutter speaks of his love

Lady, I came for your love – not to haggle.
I am no wizened mariner of orbs familiar knowledge,
But a castaway escaping the casket's clamour -
Our years wait in your mantled hourglass beyond that door,
My journey is measured in the distance to the bed head.

Strand me not here for my bones shudder to cease and the sand runs down.
I would be Warm and Content and Yours.

Madam, I am no callow stent and lack the vigour to court these months;
the days are ours and I have not the tongue to maintain the nights as once
I climbed to masthead nests and sailed high.
Put away this doubting nunnery,
turn the key, loose the handle and say you are mine.

Thunderstorm

in ancient ozonal furies
I'll be hanging around
long after I'm gone
interred or spread
steal Peter's keys or Old Nick's dement
those electric sheets
we'll kick off amidst the noise
of billowing nights or days
when the ever-baptismal rain
cries out of overflowing fonts
lightning theatre shines hills
thundering initiate stage design
our agora knows the second call
is only a curtain of restraint
growling for release from somewhere

Pablo

Who cares for the driftwood now
the dried-out pitchfork

wrapped in an old windbreaker
there on the scoured hill

weeping dried out years
ranting into the wreck of time

celestial sands bury deeper
grainy roots tether glassy contours

that anchored love's morass
or once gave safe hearth

for a while in the heat
some things are forged

Don't ask me

because what mattered
was the way the grass sang
moving the shade to watercolour
or the quiver towards a kiss
the place in your back that defines physics
a hover of breath
in the white hawk of a flat palm
waiting for lips to rise

Ballooning, Yarra Valley

On my birthday
my lover gave me flight
softly lifted in the gentle exhale of a God
over the weir wall range

below us the closed wing of our lives
a handmade throw sewn together as farms
laid out for our comfort
drifting between ecstasy and mortality

on the ground a centipede of many fingers
withdrawing its gifting rivulets
unwrapped like a towel from her hair
all in a wickerwork that lands me

over electric lines.

Three quarters of a time, coming home with the wind

before our hands had their writing paper
you dropped a pie at Victoria Park
in an unwilling flash of distraction

now our palms cannot be read
carrying all the criss crossing delta
these everglades are unmapped

but an outline of things always remains
like a photo from an orbiting satellite
the tracings under the palette board

revealed in brush and knife overlays
as specific as an exclamation mark
or hypnotic as a revolving scoreboard

tallying the points of rushes forward
scratching the old parchment tickets
the turnstiles within the pastry

the cheer squad where my sister said
you were too much woman for me
but then your empty fingers touched mine

Sunsetted Clauses

She told me
my hips could carve ham,
a girl I loved
dead early on a Sunday morning,
a car in a suburban chance roll
over the edge of Hailes Street.

Langy knows we still blame him.
His life of laying bricks
the string line's quiver
a darting mouse,
the memory of water in hay
fleeting scent of flax.

He's mixed only cordial
these foundation decades,
head too small for the mullet
drooping Frank Zappa grey.
Doesn't look a soul in the eyes,
mortar can't fill deep fissure.

DNA

there's a madman in the square
people are closing their windows
he's crying out he's found the code

of how the house smelled of oranges
when we made the almond flour cake
and the scent rained through every room

stirring in a wing flap heart beat
not the dull flat bottom skiff of ducks
slumbering off the scoria embankment

but the savage embrace of a hurtling beak
I stalled face on in mid-air unafraid
as the rushing gust pierced and passed

the skins fall away in pulsing forensics
my nose is buried in the aromatic aftermath
of how the house smelled of oranges

This is a half-done fjord/wood splitting accident blues

Erik the Blood Eye can only squint
into the sun of homecoming
casting itself out along runways,
lined with the kelp of torn out hair
of all the waiting tendrils.

Those crowning glinting wisps
shaking down into the rising fog
lifted by the gentle hand of their bequest,
the finest remembered artists
mixing their beautifully poisoned leads
into the unspoken insanity of hues.

Amethyst in ice is the colour of souls
made whole by your return.

Fado

a wine glass hums to the memory
of your laugh

lost my tongue
to your twelve-string refrain

aromas are veils
of languages over rooms no longer

familiar with dialects
where short sheeted restlessness scries
out vague tunes

a foreigner in the streets
of our house
the portuguese guitar summons

hands to hallelujah
earrings stirred for a pic
that unplayed chord knows

The Full Moon

God I loved you,
like the Antarctic ice shelf crashing
into the Great South.
Just the now of it,
how that moment was
beginning and ending
with nothing either side.

The risen full moon's yellow eye
can witness but never understand
the seamless elapsing there.
Our breath white smoke to cold air,
we stayed beneath the blanket's glamour
where time was space and space was time.

Don't wake love and burden the poor light that
modern science breaks open to reveal -
the old adage of the heart's bemoaning;
stirring would shatter the still mosaic
of such an ardent desired archaeology.

First, 1975

The first drive east. Out past dauntless new
suburbs scattered like a teenager's room.
Asleep in the future. All that aspiration watching
from the cosy dissemble of the city's embrace,
but curled like a cat, the tail flicking impatiently.
My first car. The HD station wagon
early morning, no other traffic –
the world in hibernation except for us.
Pages turned quietly in a slow read, no frantic jittery
cartoon of flipping characters, the year after colour.
Through towns only read about, where lakes enter sea
and you were talking of how your sisters
all wanted to be the first to cry 'beach'.
We promised never to have straphanger days,
travelling in a capsule of repleting dawns.

Abandoned soliloquy

a flotsam head
not quite ashore
treading water   seemingly

speaking ancient Greek or reformed Latin
who would know these days

drifting down a tidal river
to eastern beaches
water like tea

augury symptoms in urine
the lost squid in a rock pool
waiting for the afternoon tow

once hands held out arrival
for our beautiful roles
your ventriloquist's tongue
in a perfect sentence

you drove the core out
peeled my love in one long threat
the scrutiny of your beak dissecting

no boat can get anchorage
the Antarctic breath colludes
capsizing histories

all along the shipwreck coast
our children   your new young lover

hoping the mast they cling to
has a future where the baggage
intersects a stranger's journey

these serpent arms
that held your face in compromise
I licked the salt from your inner thighs
strangled ambition for a wanting
so powerful my eyes were burnt out

the estuary pushes
this infection squeezed abroad
one way a new continent

turn about   parturient islands arch
hardy shoulders curse the dozen labours

bent to the task like the trees of Patagonia

Sorting the Morning

I am waiting for day
here in the bed without you
spreadeagled on seconds
that take light years to arrive and depart.
Going over your letters and postcards
I wonder if love can be diminished in transit
so giddy I might lose myself
in the slippery travertine of words and images.
I'm volley balling the moon
pretending to focus somehow resolute
if I look at the clock and an hour has passed
then I know I'm getting there.

Free Fall

I lost you where I found you
in the barely furnished hallway
where you practised a headstand
waiting for the lift bell to signify arrival
or departure where I found you

in those nights you tasted of ocean
and somehow coriander
as you pushed yourself above me
out of those blurry ends of winter
where I found and then lost you

we skydived from this world
in a free fall of sex and language
broke formation losing grip
landing in a vacant corridor
where I lost you where I found you

Roman Baths

this morning stretch
of extracted core sample
a study of antipodes
can't assay in proof

your first kiss to my belly
that falling butterfly tapestry
or what my hand translates
in the sleuth of your back

these separate rooms
as breathing needs sleep
not to tell the children
of this old ruin you and me

where the hypocaust
intact between the villas
is stoked with more
than the occurrence of heat

Frog Love

Now so still
the pond of our bed
entwined corn fronds

before in the graceful night
I dragged a star down
planted where your head rests

years grow backwards

quietly the light is listening

walk carefully here
softly pull the wild dandelion
its poverty of flower
in all I had to give
with each tailing wind
the tremble of breeze
is me always me
so I touch you again
everything we were
in here to threads
floats an unbidden course
rises to outwit the living
smart people will say
there's more it's complicated
until a whisper can be heard

Graffiti, Fitzroy North, 1980

I couldn't understand a word of that letter
delivered in the envelope of your room
a tiny alcove posting above Rushall Crescent
while you cried throughout my incomprehension
trees forage while people salvage and the rest
better when you spoke it straight out
cutting off each finger at a time
the professor of religious studies
in his office or the tracks off surf coast beaches
and our old friend who set his feet on fire
warming them in the antique green gas oven afterwards
so long ago a day caught in gnashing cogs
stuck there grinding away shredding us to just friends
now of course the years notch and hold in place
maybe you had the right of it
I never loved you enough
perspective like graffiti gets washed away
and replaced with something else

Potter's Wheel

I saw you straight away
although you had to point yourself out
to the avid collector recalling years

you were always on my horizon love
like a maker's relief embossed on an urn
the artisan ownership engraved

by an apprentice's hand

how beauty is marked
by the young's flensing hope
cut down to the bone of broken despair

then braised for dyes to hold shape
in the overlay finish of earthenware

did I tell you I am unfinished and cracked
yet the enamel evokes a chrysalis
no matter how you hold it up to look

Happy Birthday Gutsache

I love you
like a headstand
fallingfromtrees
or a yoga pose
tremblingtohold
the way ants scramble
overasweetglass
when your hair
isamorningstormyjex
I promise to try harder not to
singabadshowerversionofGranada
that only you'll ever hear
whenyou'redancingindeepestthought
with Wittgenstein and Steinbeck

Phone Call to Sari

Hey there Hollywood in your sunglasses
the ones with the white rim,
want to come over and listen to Leonard Cohen
and Amy Winehouse some Miles Davis,
drink red wine or white if you prefer
after fourteen years next door,
it's not that big a deal to see if that look
walking back to your car when introduced,
was what I thought it might have been
I may as well ask as I'm here shimmying on my own,
because it will be fifteen years soon
and we will run out of time for this conversation.

Hellespont Queens Parade Clifton Hill

I swam the pavement straits
to be cradled in the sacristal lay
of your curling sleeplessness
furtive strokes between pontoons
of concertinaed cars in early hours
glass beads that paced anxious steps
of drizzled rainbows on cresting roads
each night in beacon times guided
embraced by window frames
strong enough then to lift myself
through return journeys
until the verdigris signal failed
stalled to breathe slipping on tram lines
hands in the air unable to inhale
the sounds of your forgiveness

Palliative Care

I'll sponge you with that moon
when the years shape my hands,
to close over the impossible
landscapes of everything we are.
The flecks of wattle gossamer
where my cheek rested,
as I listened to the Niagara rush
laughing through your belly
in those prehistoric days.
You dyed your hair jacaranda
then pomegranate, enough to confuse
the light plaiting between
the salvaged Beardsley glass panes.
Cellophane days in hidden crinkles
art nouveau flickering leaves,
tessellate our lives in Roman ways
of stones and glassy jewels.
Throw out the failing medicines
those prescriptions of what's not,
let's lay beneath the wax plant,
listen to the bees dream of everlastings.

Here and Now/Then and There

Love walks out of the same door
it came in by,
the aperture between heart and mind
be grateful for that.
How the rooms grew in adrenalin rush
and the most simple of things
a sofa for instance,
where you hugged over family life and death
held in the turmoil of it all.
Wallpaper moments that look back at you
open windows that let sighs waver,
laughter doing the washing up
whose turn it was to cook in that lousy oven.
The speeding world settled
in scattered books and music,
fur balls and muddy paws
or a child's sudden end of the world sob.
Close the panel tenderly,
turn the handle as though
you're touching a rib cage gently,
this place was the centre of something.

Out of the Bend

I took what was left within
of the things that were us
to where the river slowly
curses the incursion of willows
and out of that foreign discourse
some meaning fell a sound not speech
like the way fingers float over an ear
the slightest scrabble
writing of the once familiar
in tones of departure

Husk

this spiky chestnut thing
a skin tearer so hard to say
love or not love,
found wandering midst tidal wash
a broken shell seduced
off the rock of heaving thoughts,
made a necklace
for someone's fancy
or cat'o'nine tails fleshing,
dive into the dumping nectar
salt cleanser wile away
break the hoary mace of chain,
you only live once
that's the weary rub
but you can die of it
or live over and over again

Last Days of Watsonia High

I heard from Hooper you were dead
like whale song in watery fragments
through Donovan's harmonica

see you running down the corridor
in velvet defiance of the headmaster's
ropes to separate the sexes

that lasted as long as peace

you and Debbie chided my chauvinism
over My Lai photos that dragged barbed wire
through our country's clogged heart

that first ballet pirouetted
in teeming Swanston Street moratoriums
polished tiles skis for worn out socks

these things the apartheid of years

can't separate from a barricade relief
mixes mislabelled tea chests leaving homes
bite down on a hard spoon of distance

should have kissed that wavy dolphin Suzanne
splashing behind your knee

One year I grew Navajo maize

kernels of a jeweller's dream
sacred as the psalms of Solomon,
when the waking day rippled

they shone louder than hearsay,
of a pain so bewildering and lost
the sheathes sobbed a melancholy

and all season by broken night
the thud of other falling fruit,
made steps outside of conscience.

Within my pawn shopped love
is too solemn a precipice,
a girder in cantilever out over

an empty gallery hanging space,
where bricks slowly isolate
the sound of a facade crashing,

but those hesitant frontiers cling
their plating portraits hidden,
hopeful as a seed between lips.

Diary of Anne Boleyn

My ladies weep in the vernacular tongue
kneeling in the French style

I caught the wren as another's head fell
and later perched for witness

at the place near the abbey a heartbeat quiet
then loud the cat still as sculpture

artful ferocity in those bloody sinew lines
drew from these palms a sanctuary

a censer swings slowly for a thousand days
the metal clanging its catechism

open hands meet the knowledge of ravens
given voice from a wooden block

release an olive complexion by Wyatt written
in pulse of reformist contraband

arms drop at side outstretched fingers release
not falconry or master's quiver

took flight a stalked harmless precious thing
away from the predator and papal manoeuvring

a scavenge of royal alchemists pecks to parts
the once kindest knit of souls

the loins of a king are as common as any man
tempested wings erupt impatient there

On the Death of a Past Love

The honey in your hair mixed
morning's brew, that old cassette player
held us suspended, above lanes weaved
by another century. I would go back,
knowing it was my turn to change the tape
fix the twist with a pencil.

All noise is a rib cage, a trapped soloist
weeps out of tune, how the world rose grating
then, against a lidless basket of us.
We had our best before date
when my feet marched flat against the Draft
but my hands found you.

I don't know what to say

when I find a strand of your hair
over a chair like a ribbon

or the silk that holds me for a second
walking between the old orchard trees

I lay it back in place there

you'd laugh over that fastidious detail
how it must be undisturbed

and you would slightly bite my shoulder
as I came back up to protest

all elocution compressed in that nibble

sometimes waking not realizing the cat sighs
in the crossways where you dreamed

one day she'll have to know
quietly as a lost breeze surfacing

but I don't know what to say

not Another small Fucking love Poem

This is how love ends:
I couldn't get anything right
And I gave up trying at all.
Stuck like a dinghy out past
The breakers waiting to come in.
Watching you shoeless on the beach,
Annoyed at the sand I've become
Between your toes irritating
When it used to be a tickling joy.
My voice a curlew now
Unmoving in the fog,
Persistent though like Archimedes' principle
Held up in my hand hoping
For one more pass by the sand bar.

I Have Your Back

This is a poem in black and white
a 'noir' piece of hoped impress,
not a lino cut from a gallery I can't afford.

As an ear pressed to a shell
in the small of your back,
I hear waves running to colour arrival.
My palm read by inner thigh
all the truth of Heart and Life lines
leave footprints in the wet sand
for the pounding surf to collect.

Wandering the estuary,
I know where we are
I can always see this.

My Stammer Art

You and me
could be us
if not for a stutter
over words like
fffffffforever
we could endure
persist like budding
tarragon after snow
or hair over eyes
fffffffinally
avoiding the don'ts
of separate lives
be dots stuck on
exclamation marks
fffffffree

I span in a hammock

that your father had hung
between the silver birches
stooping copsed guardians

imitating a graceful deference

yet the sky turned with me
and spilled me there
embarrassed a little shaky

still able to do a push up

while the family cat smirked
and a smiley dog licked the blood
from my forehead

later when no one looked

you first kissed the gravel away
then coming over the next day
the hammock was folded on the porch

under the cockatiel cage

Gyp your Labrador heeler cross
scraped a rear leg over new stumps
but I hadn't washed my head

life's a bit like that

Bequeathable Sanitoria

Don't be offended
if as an old love song

you're the needle in my arm
the messy heart and anchor tattoo

that won't be scratched out
of these polished corridors

locked down night and day
awaiting the scuff of attendants

as they whistle away
'hear, I'm going back to Massachusetts'

you're the straightjacket
I can't shake loose of

borrowed shoes for romance
not enough hair for style

out of the high storey window
my second-hand jacket open

phalanger spread flying cover
the last cast iron bed home

if you were there to hold me
in a wayward parable of rain.

Made in Milk

The cattle have grazed through the wait
anxious at the gate getting noisy
throwing heads shuffling feet in the dark
udders tight with the thought of grain

this winter icy frigid as despair
in your hair a faint elixir of that secret smoke
the pack of Old Jamaica you hide
behind the grease gun where I don't go

enough rain to bring in Spring dams full
if you must get up I'll have early lunch ready
a special gourmet treat from my menu of eleven
probably number three the Mexican beans

although I'd rather you stayed awhile
listening to the river play La Nina's nocturne
there's nothing unknown to discover outside
under these blankets it's as warm as hello.

I wore a day as showy as

The Wonga vine is late
this long Spring year

like drunken party guests
who finally arrive
in tumbling blowsy silk

dancing a too close Latin
manes tangled in the distance
parted by a cigarette paper

(although we've heard
about the separation)

a vicarage of noisy miner birds
tries to chaperone
their pursed censure all bravado

as others depart slowly
pretending not to watch.

Love breaks

one way then the other
an undertow without misgivings
unpatrolled no warning signs

a catching spilling embrace
lifts and throws all in one action
bends to snap strands to beach

in between lowered flags
you loll on memoir fringes
a hand signals covets the light

rinse the grainy suds out
more than a toe in hurl forward
that taste in your mouth is hope

I'll lay down with dictionaries (and you)

When we are too old
for the Crossword
and the swallow comes early
singing for a lost partner

when out of season
the whip bird's tuning fork
calls the humble circle
out of a lasso's embrace

sky writing your name
in that opened portal
vowels and consonants
placed inside the circumference

dangling missing letters
we have chanced for canvass
a wily clue you gave me
of secrets no one knows

lexicons hesitantly shelved
the answers between us
teased into definition
out of more solitary lives

then leave all pages open
make a cuneiform mattress
out of every alphabet
graft us to our own calligraphy

the words that seek homes
can pummel for new comfort
rub against us until found
here where our language formed

Letter to Lois

I've experienced falling
but never in such a tumble

twirling like a tin can

I wanted to tell you
without the safety
of a cloak's heightened perspective

how much I love
your human fragility

the joy in a wind chime

to feel the scissor depth of an ending
the gothic pages of ink

newsprint wrapping a bouquet

the short speech of balloons
a stagey mess of comic action figurines

tell Jimmy my favourite one
is still you and me in mufti
holding out our Press cards
the ill-fitting fake lenses
my gin to your tonic

and I'm now way past
the speed of time's sight

where our shape has no dimension
holding on to this cobalt krypto rock
because I don't want the super power

of living without you forever

In Charles Street Greensborough

did my first love live
the road was unpaved
two brown kelpies paroled
honking their vigilant duty

we had coffee before school
that was all I needed then
now I hear she has died
like the phone calls I'd make

and hang up before answered
still I think of the life
we may have had together
a tumbledown waterfall

where what never happened
hauls the taut hopeful line in
a skirmish of unreconciled chance
bidding against the best years

in scratching into the scruff
behind those wondering alert ears
opaque as closed delicate eyelids
when you walk by into the future

age of the Sargasso tiger

I thought love was younger
yet it prowls through years
the swish not care or annoyance

a purring of sarcenet decades
in gentle stumble of loose wrack

the predator's teeth at your throat
incisors anything and everything
the warm blood ungated

stripes on a wisdom tooth
all in cursive hand

drop the petals of spongy knap
the wind is growling
a whirligig of castanets

Near Death (Experienced Applicants Only)
Please Address the Selection Criteria

Have you used Viagra in the past 24 hours
the paramedic asks slightly embarrassed
I answer No but is there a box
for I wish I had a reason to you can tick
while something won't dissolve
under my tongue if death comes here
more than an hour to the nearest hospital
strapped down how foreign the paisley gums
out the back in the mist are every bump
on the logger's track a cry from
a pulping tree I have no risk factors
the driver's losing traction stopping
for another reading but it's all good
then just take this in case anyway
everyone in the emergency department
is pregnant except for Andrew
I answer the same questions every time
they take blood and a reading and x ray
he tells me in Vietnam his uncle
gave him a smoke when he was four
I ask for his uncle's number for a word
our joke of me dealing with a bad relative
chuckles around Mario who's a gondolier
with a speedy trolley strokes a pole less skill
between the traffic of cubicles as he lands
me back with Paula and Nina who pull
the patches off we laugh about my flokati
chest never looking the same again
Dr Van tells me I've got a real good heart

there waiting for the all clear all I can think about
is the birth of my children how love tastes
like the bubbles in honeycomb and will my hand
ever slowly take a cast of your hip again

Leary Presents at the Writers Festival

(In this world/
love has no colour –
/yet how deeply/
my body/
is stained by yours)
Izumi

What remains struggles for the hand grip of language, the shake of letters, the whirly get you moment of transparency in this ever-expanding universe of no departure intersect indifferent to the eternity of loss, and how he draws a profile in any reflective surface, through all grains of furniture. Undisturbed by answers, a scent of daily grief, the vanilla of her vapour trail sky writing in every hotel shower.

The M.C will introduce him, still living off his seminal 'Aspects of the Aesthetic Dialectic between Long and Short Prose - the Powershift of Form'. It chased him down, that title, the whippet pack of ideas to his skinny frantic rabbit, wanting to join Alice or Aesop, disappear into a picture edition fable. His working title 'Barbed Wire in the Soul – a Treatise of Meaning' unacceptable.

Leary pretends to be attentive, shuffles papers, now in larger typeface, tries not to pick his nose, or do that ear thing Marjorie complained about. Soon there will have to be a beginning, but his armpits are itchy, and concentrating on the front row, all he can think about are piano keys and how sitting is an unnatural algorithm, a human is more of a tightened spring, no wonder then that people have back problems or fucking haiku.

Fucking haiku, flash fiction, found fucking plagiarism, discovered poetry, witnessed presence, closing in, this oily slick of a black hole, each syllable putting out another light, quenching meaning, dragging down silhouettes. There's some mirth in the audience, a joke about that Title, a quip about models and electronic start. He puts on the appreciative smile, the knowing in joke, the clown's cosmos enlightened by occasional surprise.

Leary knows soon there will have to be a beginning, but fifteen dollars for a fucking chapbook, stapled with tetanus and bloodied fingerprints. A slow soft hammer of depth through the temples, resounding in afterthought, a volume you can get a bookmark in, or remember the page number chapters later, a handwritten line you keep beside the chair, twenty-five dollars of light years.

A Plenary Session, a stage, there'll be questions. His short piece should be to the point. Enough to tantalise, provoke, not offend. His notes are becoming origami, his fingers holding kite strings, the meniscus between earth and that fucking dialectic cumuli brain matter eroding. Dressed in clandestine hunger a Greek eats de lapin with sage and onion sauce, fish get their scales by weighing submerged thought.

Leary knows she's a xanthous year in decades a saffron ticking weapons grade love that is metered in care of oats the flowing in plainsongs all intimacies drawn to the sane touch of palms reading lines of shale coast mourning departures by fountain pen gifts to breach the past. The imprint of gesture when she waved away his idiosyncrasies, dropped the commas from his tongue, closed his mouth with lips out of reason.

Death defying chance comes uninvited paradigm of genius and clothes of the Imperial Court kimono courtesan love abridged between centuries trees felled for pages a big bang created all birth truth is found in the deceit of clay feet in synopsis is interred breadth her absence in every room.

He is being introduced, and he knows there is a beginning for every conclusion, as short or as long as every fucking haiku, written in a Komachi or Shikibu smile.

Into the Wilderness

we lived without time then
when Lake St Clair blew to waves

that cabin luxury for us
wood table and chairs
the bunk off the floor

I was reading
Crime and Punishment
too young for temptation

we loved each other
no regret beneath our tan lines

in those days I could eat
a whole loaf and honey

the visiting heron had no song
in the rounds of its silent joy
just the thwack of happiness

you said I should read
The Ginger Man
while holding Jean-Paul's trilogy

Leonard Cohen and Me, Not by the Levee

In a cruciform town
built of stone and sweat
they laid us both down
for the crime of theft

we swam ourselves naked
shook a fist at the moon
where the oily anointed
are past dead too soon

> *that's what you get baby*
> *for wanting to be free*
> *that's what you get baby*
> *for wanting to be free*

I kissed tattooed children
their faceless smiles also
way beyond the power of ten
there on your blessed torso

they came in the night
too afraid of the day
a list of what was right
their fears to allay

> *and that's what we got baby*
> *for wanting to be free*
> *and that's what we got baby*
> *for wanting to be free*

our bodies are our irony
a scorn of deliberate charade
away from that cold cold valley
the fulcrum of us was made

we stole the lonely chastity
giving everything we had
they told us it was blasphemy
go tell them we were glad

> *and that's what we got baby*
> *for wanting to be free*
> *and that's what we got baby*
> *between you and me*

Now I'm Sixty-Four

Summer holiday morning, our town an
overfull éclair. Dogs on leave
bark for home, and teenagers rev the engines
of older family members. Visiting cats
wander into other territories, the wattle birds,
all rusty complaint, while the rooster has crowed
its night long displacement. The heatwave hums
along with coolers, the air as heavy as a cold
you can't shake. We used to hear the ocean,
but now the incessant northerly owns us all.
Still, here I am, at the most honest point in life,
having passed the age of knowing, and sure
of who we are, on the second cup of coffee.
If reincarnation is true, I want to come back
to this point with you, the rest of our lives
secure from past loss, and this stable present
a buoy in any current. Things can go along,
float around us, music has captured hours,
streams happy or sad decades, becoming
calm arrival. You tell me the French call
this La Petite Mort; I don't know what time
it is, or what day. Like watching the ocean,
or an open fire, becoming selfless as seasons.
We're as tactile as stucco, my hand
on your wrist, your fingers on my collar bone,
the sensation of a sherbet dusting.

Kissing Helen Mirren

There was some traffic today
a car came down the Yarragon road
although I waited throughout the drizzle

no return occurred

wasps strummed navigating the pears
and I thought I heard voices
but it was only the gossip of birds

talking of Ray who died of liver failure

he made me copies of old LPs
and told of how he kissed Helen Mirren
at a London nightclub in 1969

I didn't go to the funeral

perhaps he peaked too soon
but I know the blissful point
of melting ice cream happens

and how orange cordial mixed with ice
wound up like an elastic stringed ball
bounces around in your chest

Rap, rap, rap, rap, ill tidings call

It came like rain on windows
a specimen in a jar,
the lid too tight for breathing.
I fumbled through the program
how those Austrians can dance,
but it was only distraction.
Among the seals from Kaikoura
the black sand of carbon footprints,
your South Island smile.
Brushing your hair at the station
how it fell fell fell fell,
my hands these brittle things.
Only yesterday I cleaned the drawers
the orange oil won't let go,
sorting through the ones to send you.
The old farm by Tarra Valley Road
tree ferns bowed down after snow,
the forever of a late Winter's day.
I've spread them out like a Tarot Patience
readings given brazed futures unheld,
tenets of lapsed things holding to landscape.
Now they have nowhere to go
caught as they are in the what of it,
while I think on the eulogy your children ask for.

But my lips digress

at the place I turn a cheek to
between anatomy of hip and certainty
where science and faith untangle

tongues discover all languages
in that sweeping terrain
each vertebrae a patent

your secrets safe there
my heart folding out of office
in the finest drafting

gender less in ways sculptors see

Wuthering

for a while
I was Cathy
and that knocking
was your return

      because pain has no gender

its seeking ways of counterpoint
slim branches on the window
wispy enough getting through
the social veneer of a card house teeter

      your breath held within mine

from the firebox
the slow drumming
still so young all wings

nothing gained by asking
it fell to this place
took the day when offered

      lost the latch key of reason

resumes by night confused
upon release it hovers
browses Christmas lights
as any honeyeater might

    although your hands
      were gentle enough for rescue

before waking again
to deconstruct this dangerous allure
our palms all moony on the glass

    cupped enough to settle here

Truman Capote's brownstone

Holly's voice
fingers digging between ribs
the one-eyed cat's
zig zag troupe

the shower running

after the call up
rooms full of old grey white men
in avalanche
interring country and western songs

a guitar taut as strung throats

no one's Fred
callow as a phone booth at Joe Bell's
should have listened sooner
a false note on every dollar

in old Spanish towns they believed
blindness gave voice a tone
birdcage on a sidewalk

a marmalade rescue
warming a window
awash in a cul de sac

our histories gutter up
perhaps for snow or fire
the past best kept as fine china

That's all, folks

these mornings my dreams
seem to lack production values

on the asphalt in the back lot
the noir misplaced
uneven between the scenes

the director's chair
blown against an earlier century

waiting for that new kid
chewing words at an angle
confident that the world

understands the lines

a lone sparrow drifting
making feast of scattered crumbs

then the ocean's tracer light
soundtracks of distant bikes
revs through the outland of dawn

a crew rustling for breakfast

the waves as near as skin
you singing in your sleep
those big band auditions

bringing in technicolour

Acknowledgements

Many of these poems, sometimes in a slightly different version, have appeared in:

- *The Emma Press Anthology of Love* – Edited by Rachel Piercey and Emma Wright
- *Australian Love Poems* – edited by Mark Tredinnick
- *Anti Heroin Chic*
- *The Lake*
- *Poetry d'Amour Anthology* 2014
- *Poetry d'Amour Anthology* 2017 – Edited by Kevin Gillam,
- *Persian Sugar in English Tea* – Edited by Soodabeh Saeidnia and Aimal Zaman Yusufzai
- *Your One Phone Call*
- *The Blog Project 365+ One*
- *Hubgarden*
- *Bluepepper*
- *Glasgow Review of Books*
- *The Leviathan's Apprentice* 2015
- *Museo de la Palabra*
- *Silver Birch Press*
- *Contour Magazine – The Love Edition*
- *Somnia.blue*
- *North of Oxford*
- *antinarrative journal*
- *The Ugly Writers*
- *Australian Poetry Journal Members Anthology*
- *Indolent Books*
- *Svensk Apache*
- *Wild Word*

- *Outlaw Poetry*
- *Peace Tolerance and Understanding Poems from the ACU 2015 Prize for Poetry*
- *Nerdalicious*
- *Academy of the heart and mind*
- *Australian Latino Press*
- *The Rye Whiskey Review*
- *Ramingo's Porch*
- *The Pangolin Review*
- *Coral Press New York*
- *The Poets' Republic*
- *Lethe Literary and Art Journal*
- *The Blue Nib* and
- The Raw Art Review: *A Journal of Storm and Urge*

About the author

James Walton was a Librarian, a farm worker, and mostly a public sector union official. He is published in many anthologies, newspapers, and journals.

In 1959 he won a plastic hair brush in an art competition. His drawing of a cow won best drawing of a bull, in a school art contest.

He has been shortlisted for the ACU National Literature Prize, The James Tate Prize, Jupiter Artland, the MPU International Poetry Prize, and is a winner of the Raw Art Review Chapbook Contest 2019.

He resigned from an elected union position five years ago, and has been writing since then.

This is his third collection.

Also by James Walton:

The Leviathan's Apprentice
(Publish and Print U.K. 2015)

Walking Through Fences
(Flying Island Books ASM & Cerberus 2018)

www.ingramcontent.com/pod-product-compliance
Lightning Source LLC
Chambersburg PA
CBHW071006080526
44587CB00015B/2366